BOOK 2

Palmer-Hughes
ACCORDION COURSE

by Bill Palmer and Bill Hughes

This book belongs to____________________

My teacher is____________________

I began this book____________________

FOREWORD

The purpose of this Course is to:

1. Create and maintain interest while promoting thorough understanding and good musicianship.
2. Effectively bridge the gap between the beginner and intermediate stages as smoothly as possible.
3. Sustain the student's interest by offering a selection of material high in entertainment as well as musical value.

NOTE TO TEACHERS

The student beginning Book Two of the PALMER-HUGHES Accordion Course should be equipped with a 120 bass accordion.

This will allow the student to use the review section of Book Two to orient himself to the larger sized instrument. Since no new notes are introduced for the first 16 pages of Book Two, the student will find it very advantageous to use this period to become accustomed to handling the new instrument, without concerning himself with the problems of locating new notes.

To use the 12 bass accordion beyond page 33 is impossible, since the student must begin the use of the minor chord at this point. The student who waits until this point to equip himself with the larger instrument will of course be required to review the first part of the book before proceeding onward.

The Publishers

contents

TREBLE KEYBOARD

Of the 120 Bass Accordion

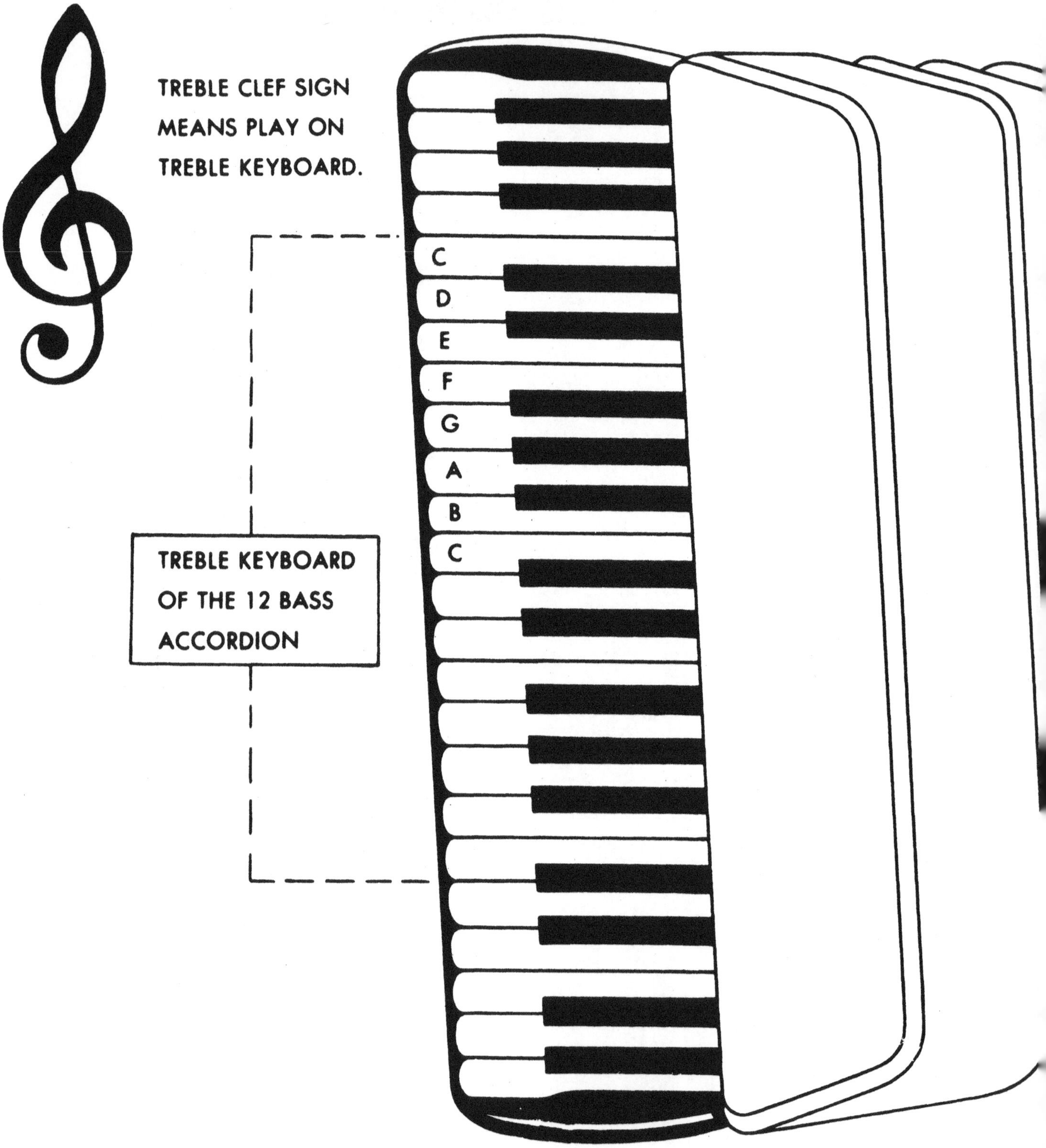

BASS KEYBOARD

Of the 120 Bass Accordion

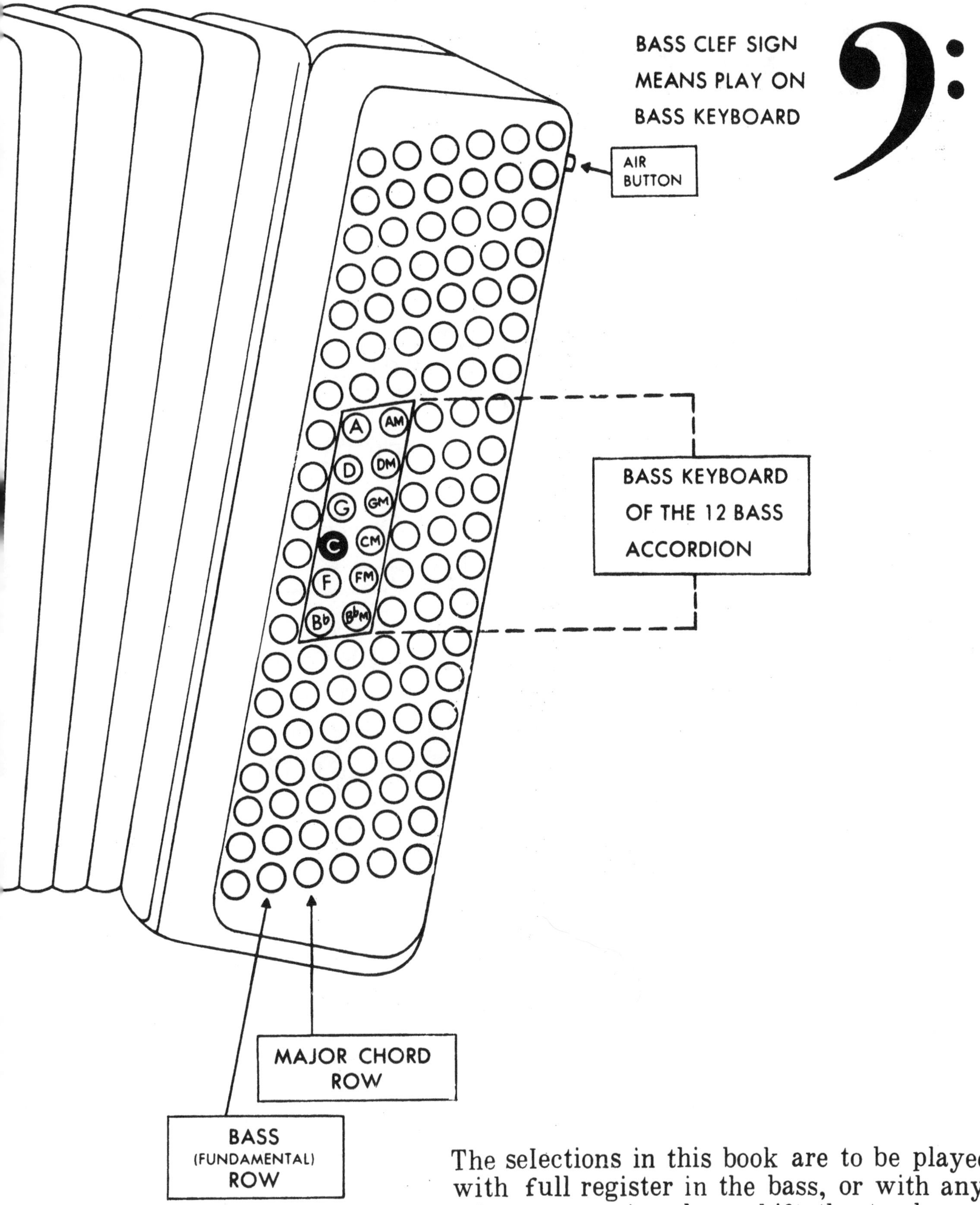

The selections in this book are to be played with full register in the bass, or with any other appropriate bass shift the teacher may recommend.

REVIEW OF THE RIGHT HAND

-TREBLE KEYBOARD OF 120 BASS ACCORDION-

TREBLE KEYBOARD OF 12 BASS ACCORDION

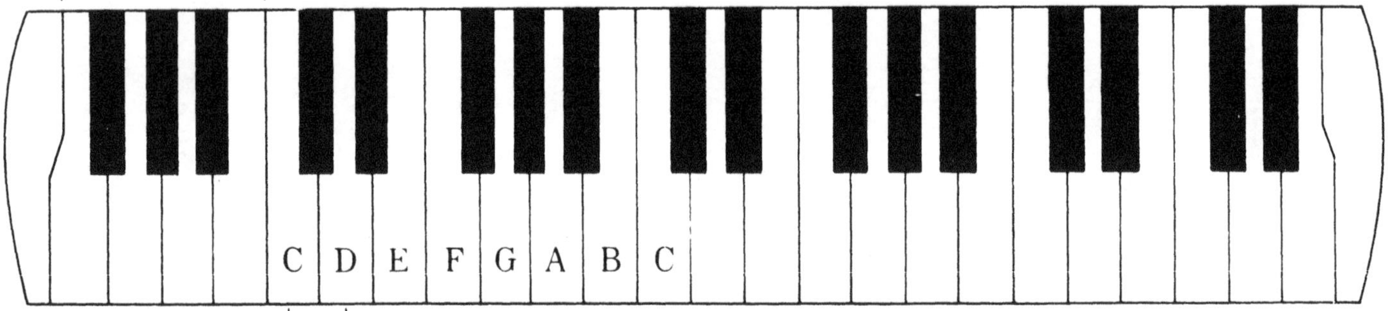

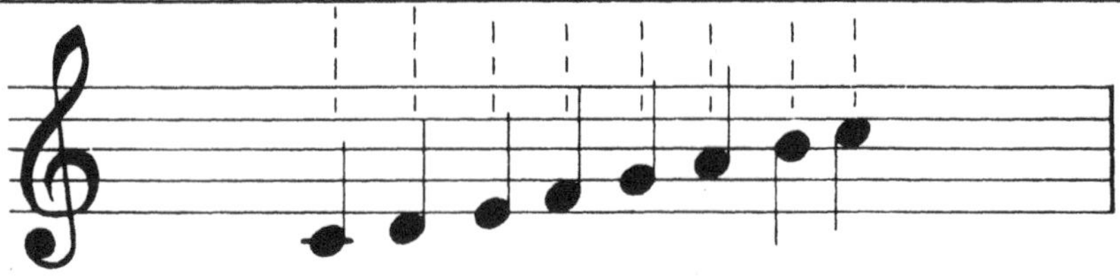

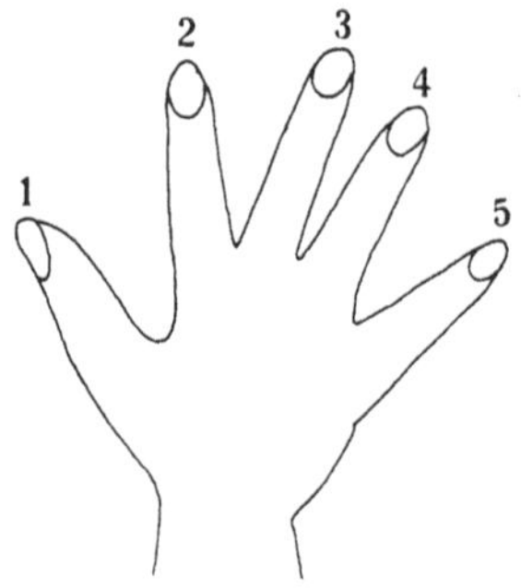

RIGHT HAND FINGERING.

REVIEW OF REST VALUES

𝄽=QUARTER REST - ONE COUNT — 𝄼=HALF REST - TWO COUNTS

𝄻=WHOLE REST - REST A FULL MEASURE OR FOUR COUNTS

REVIEW OF NOTE VALUES

A QUARTER NOTE ♩ gets ONE count.

A HALF NOTE 𝅗𝅥 gets TWO counts.

A DOTTED HALF NOTE 𝅗𝅥. gets THREE counts.

A WHOLE NOTE 𝅝 gets FOUR counts.

THE GRAND STAFF:

THE TIME SIGNATURE:

Upper number indicates FOUR counts in each measure.

Lower number indicates that a QUARTER NOTE gets one count.

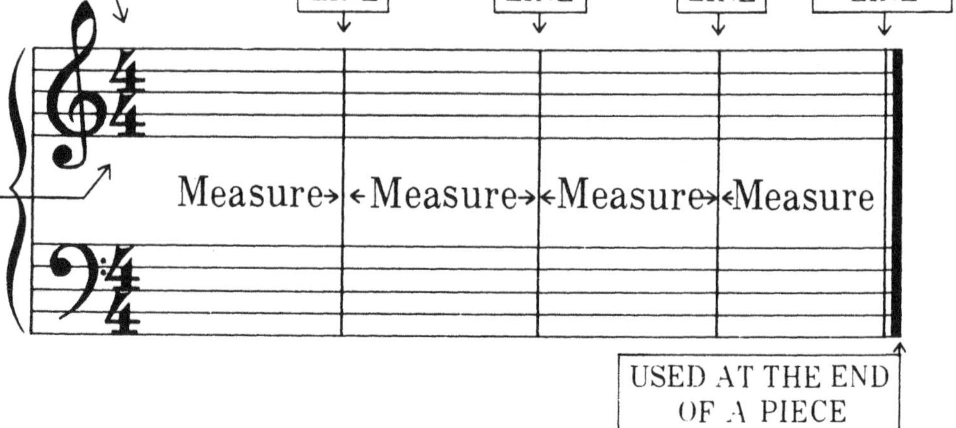

USED AT THE END OF A PIECE OR A SECTION

TREBLE STUDY:

PLAY and COUNT:

REVIEW OF THE LEFT HAND

Notes Written Above The Middle Line Are Chords

Notes Written Below The Middle Line Are Basses

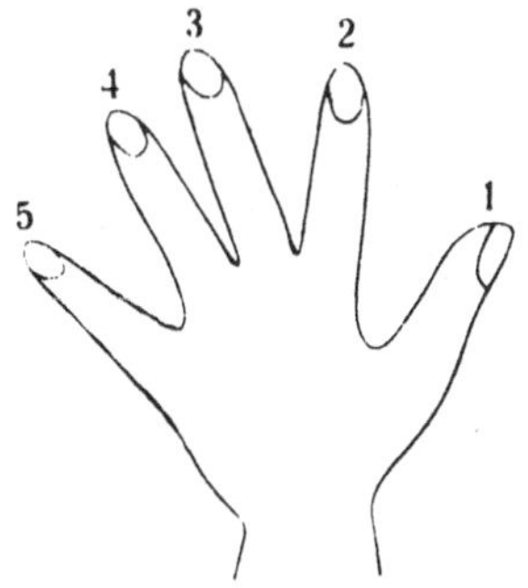

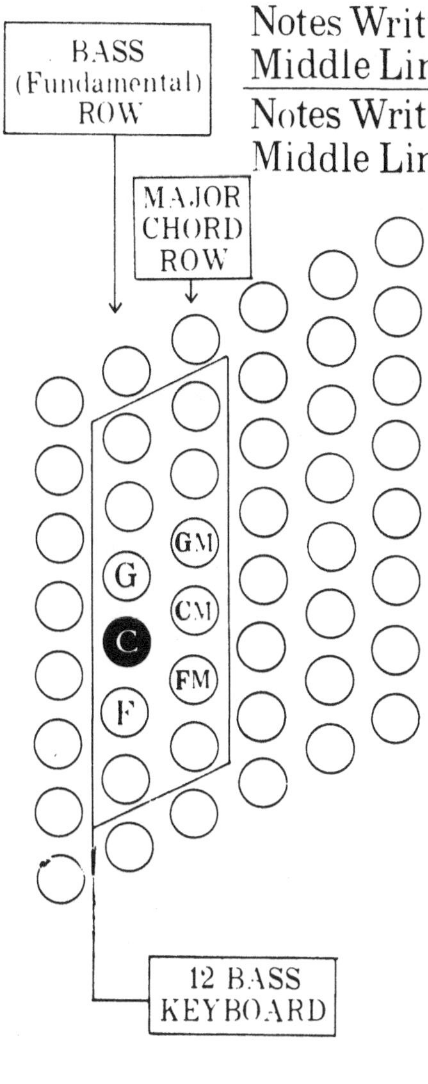

LEFT HAND FINGERING

THE REMAINING BASSES COVERED IN BOOK ONE WILL BE REVIEWED IN THE SELECTIONS TO FOLLOW.

DRINK TO ME ONLY WITH THINE EYES

Moderately slow

ENGLISH AIR

*A curved line ⌒ joining two notes on the same line or space is called a TIE. TIED notes are HELD DOWN for the time value of both notes, NOT REPEATED.

CAMPTOWN RACES

REPEAT SIGNS 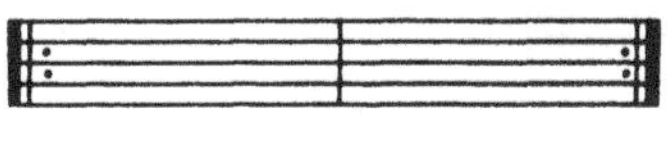 The double dots inside the double bars indicate that everything between the double bars must be REPEATED.

ALTERNATING THE BASSES

March time

Palmer-Hughes

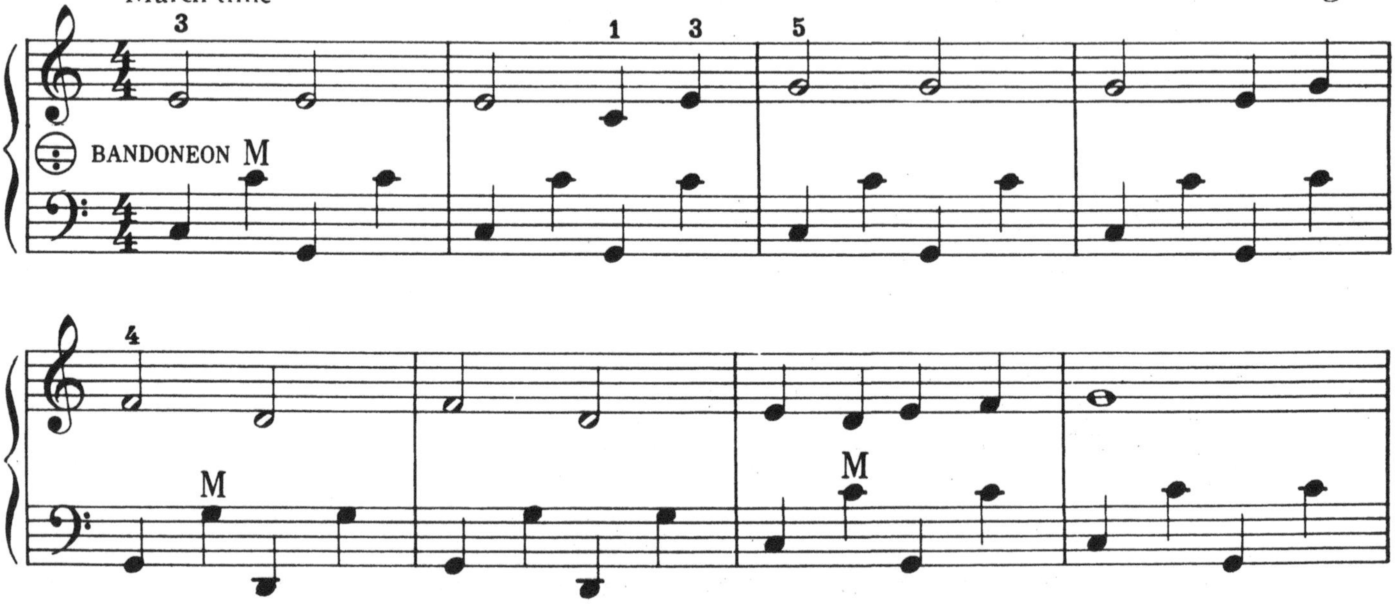

D. C. al Fine: abbreviation for "DA CAPO al Fine". Repeat from the very beginning of the selection and play to the word FINE (end).

THE CAISSONS GO ROLLING ALONG

March time

E. C. GRUBER

ACCENTS: Every measure of music should have a slight ACCENT on the first count. This is produced by applying more pressure to the bellows. This is especially true of pieces of a rhythmic nature, such as marches, polkas, waltzes, etc.

COME TO THE SEA

(VIENI SUL MAR)

A curved line ⁀ placed over two or more different notes is called a SLUR. SLURS divide the music into PHRASES (musical sentences) and indicate that the notes are to be CONNECTED SMOOTHLY.

MARINE'S HYMN

American Air

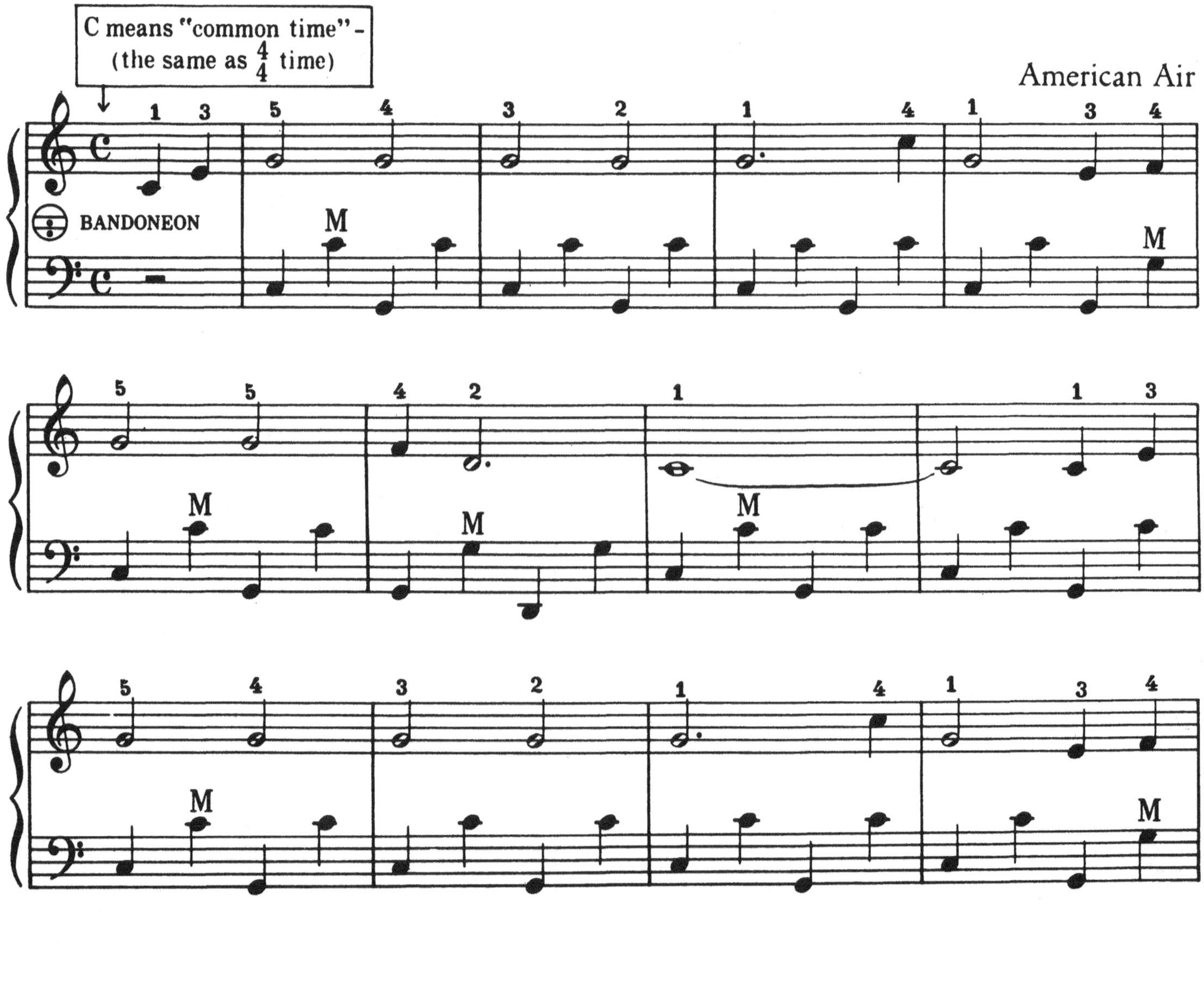

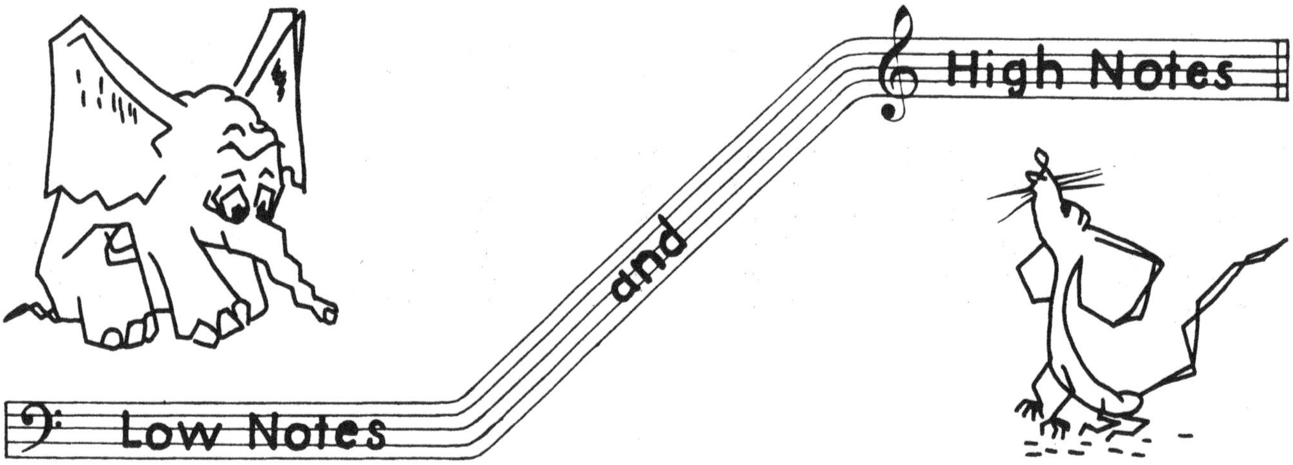

Some notes sound Low, some sound High. Can you tell the difference?

Play and Listen

The Highest notes are those
Written Highest on the staff

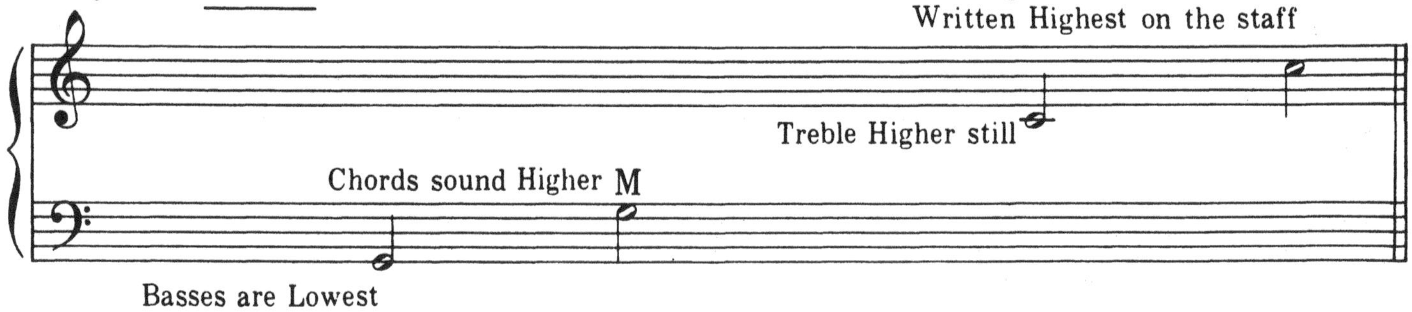

RECOGNIZING KEYS BY BLACK KEY GROUPS

Notice that the treble keyboard has groups of TWO BLACK KEYS and groups of THREE BLACK KEYS.

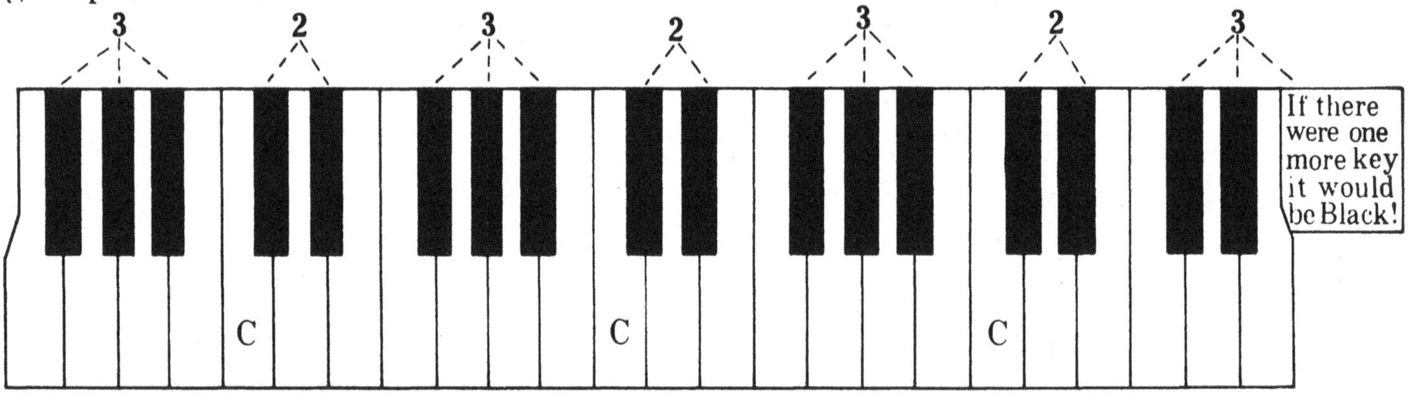

There are three C's on your treble keyboard.
Each C is to the LEFT of the TWO BLACK KEY GROUP!
Find all the C's on your keyboard!
What note is to the LEFT of the THREE BLACK KEY group? . . . .
How many of these notes are on your accordion? . . . .
Find them all on your keyboard!

What note is to the RIGHT of the TWO BLACK KEY group? . . . . .
What note is to the RIGHT of the THREE BLACK KEY group? . . . .
What note is in the MIDDLE of the TWO BLACK KEY group? . . . .
What two notes are in the MIDDLE of the THREE BLACK group? . . .

FIND ALL OF THESE NOTES ON YOUR KEYBOARD.

A HIGHER "C" POSITION

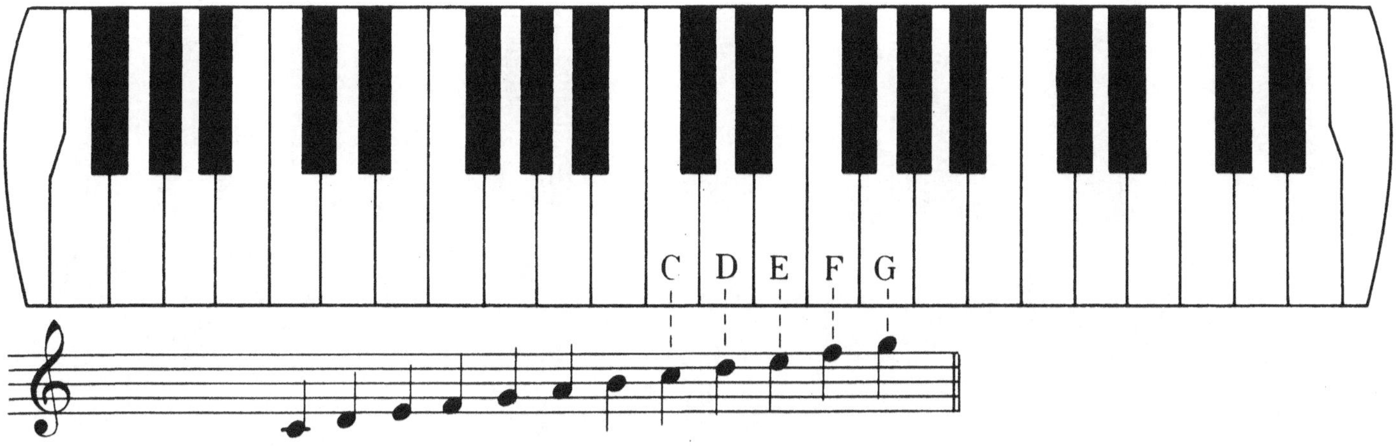

PLAY:

SPEED DRILL NO. 1

From this point on we will have speed drills. They should be practiced daily. These are very famous exercises. They were written by C. L. Hanon, and are used by the finest musicians in the world to develop speed and technique.

Start all speed drills very slowly, then gradually increase speed. Be sure that each note is clear and distinct.

Moderately slow

Franz Behr
(adapted)

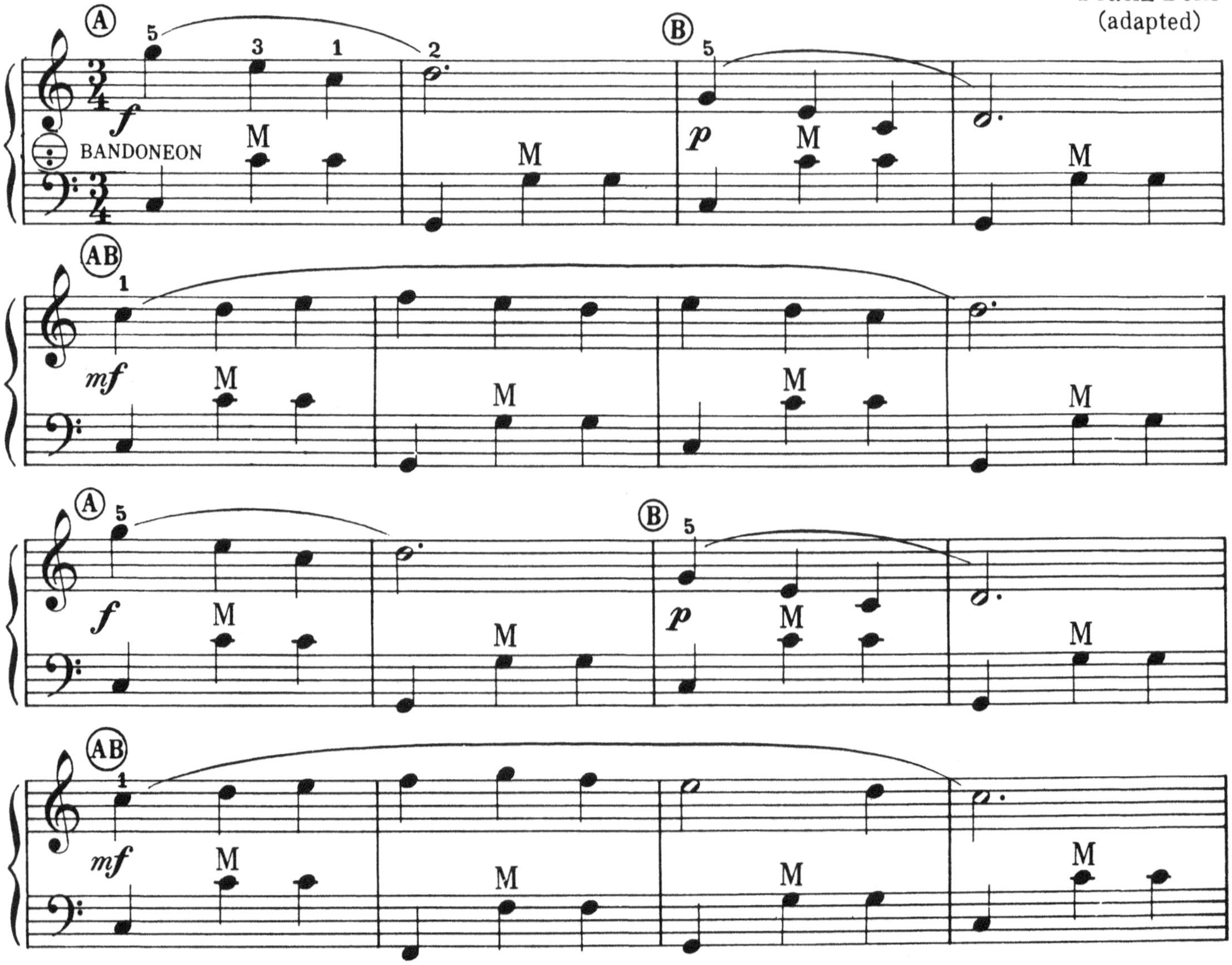

"EXPRESSION" MARKS:

f (forte) = LOUD   ***p*** (piano) = SOFT

mf (mezzo-forte) = moderately loud

For class work, the class may be divided into two groups, Group A and Group B. Measures marked "A" are played by group "A"; measures marked "B" are played by group "B". Measures marked "AB" are played by both groups.

VIVE L' AMOUR

(HOORAY FOR LOVE!)

FIRST OR SOLO PART:

COLLEGE SONG

Lively

*Notes marked WITH ACCENT MARKS receive special emphasis. This is produced by applying greater pressure to the bellows

VIVE L'AMOUR
(SECOND PART)

NOTE READING REVIEW

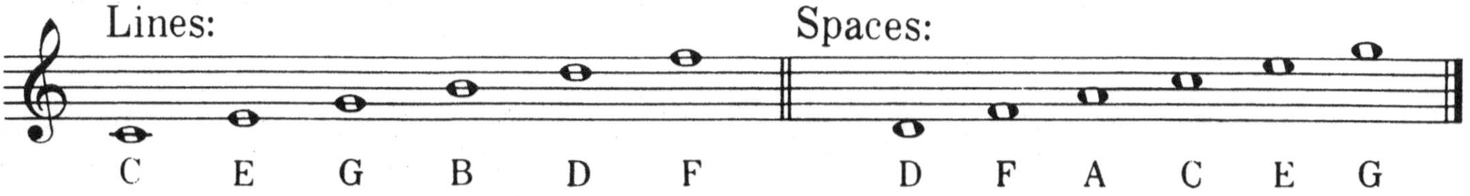

PLAY all of the following notes, saying the name of each note ALOUD, then write the name under each note:

BE CAREFUL! Watch for traps!

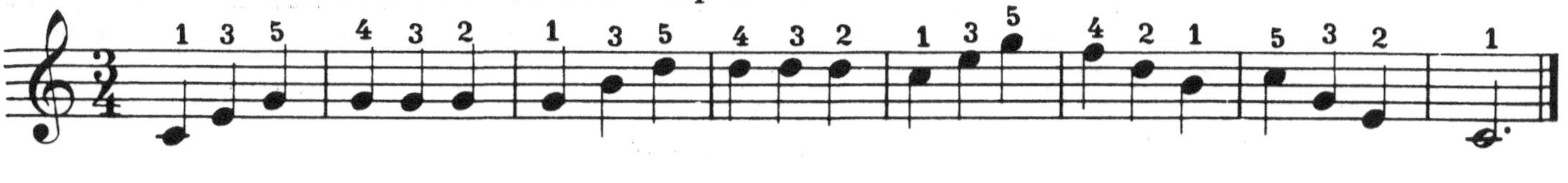

SHE'LL BE COMIN' 'ROUND THE MOUNTAIN

*DOUBLE NOTES
Lively
BAND.
She'll be com-in' 'round the moun-tain when she comes, HONK! HONK! She'll be
com-in' 'round the moun-tain when she comes, HONK! HONK! She'll be
com-in' 'round the moun-tain, She'll be com-in' 'round the moun-tain, She'll be
com-in' 'round the moun-tain when she comes. HONK! HONK!

EXTRA VERSES:

2. She'll be drivin' six white horses when she comes, WHOA! HOSS! (etc.)
3. We will all go out to meet her when she comes, HI BABE!
4. She'll be wearin' her red flannels when she comes, SCRATCH! SCRATCH!
5. We will kill the old red rooster when she comes, CHOP! CHOP!
6. We will all have chicken dumplin's when she comes, YUM! YUM!
7. She will have to sleep with Gran'ma when she comes, (snore-whistle).
8. She'll be comin' 'round the mountain when she comes, HONK! HONK!

 A two note chord, sometimes called "double notes". Strike the two keys TOGETHER.

♯ SHARPS, ♭ FLATS, and ♮ NATURALS

The distance from any treble key to the very next key, right or left, black or white, is a HALF STEP.
TWO half steps make a WHOLE STEP.

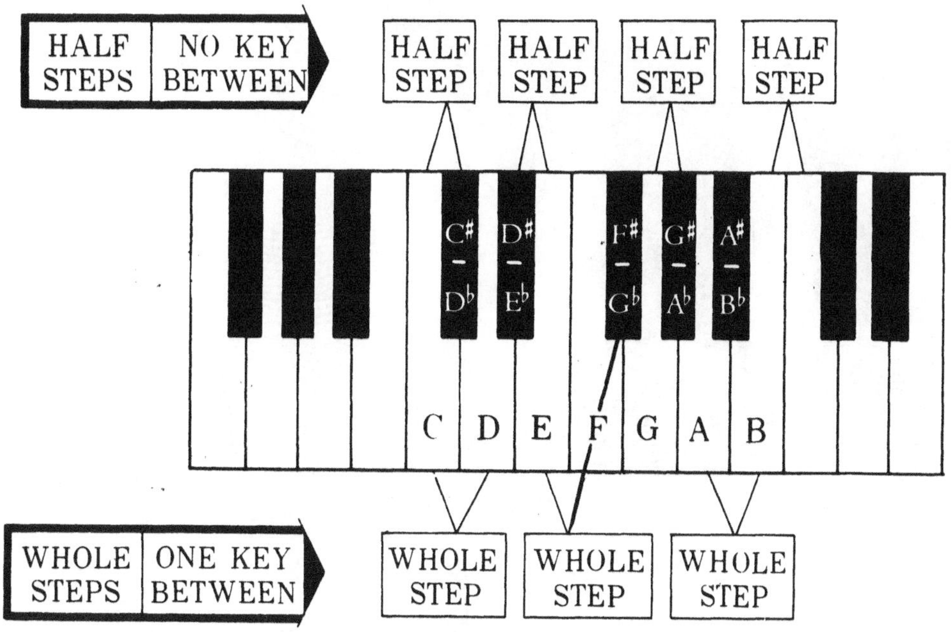

A SHARP (♯) RAISES the note a half step. Play the next key to the RIGHT.	♯

A FLAT (♭) LOWERS the note a half step. Play the next key to the LEFT.	♭

A NATURAL (♮) CANCELS a previous ♯ or ♭. A natural is ALWAYS a WHITE KEY.	♮

Locate the following notes on the Keyboard:

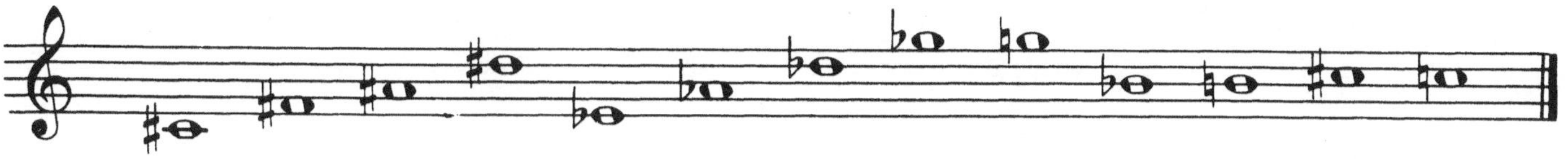

OVER THE WAVES

(Crescendo) gradually LOUDER. (Decrescendo) gradually SOFTER.

* 8va (OCTAVE SIGN). All notes under this sign should be played one octave (eight notes) higher.

INTRODUCING EIGHTH NOTES

These are EIGHTH NOTES

When one eighth note appears alone, it looks like this: or

When two or more eighth notes appear together, they look like this:

> AN EIGHTH NOTE is HALF as long as a quarter note.
> Play TWO EIGHTH NOTES to ONE COUNT.

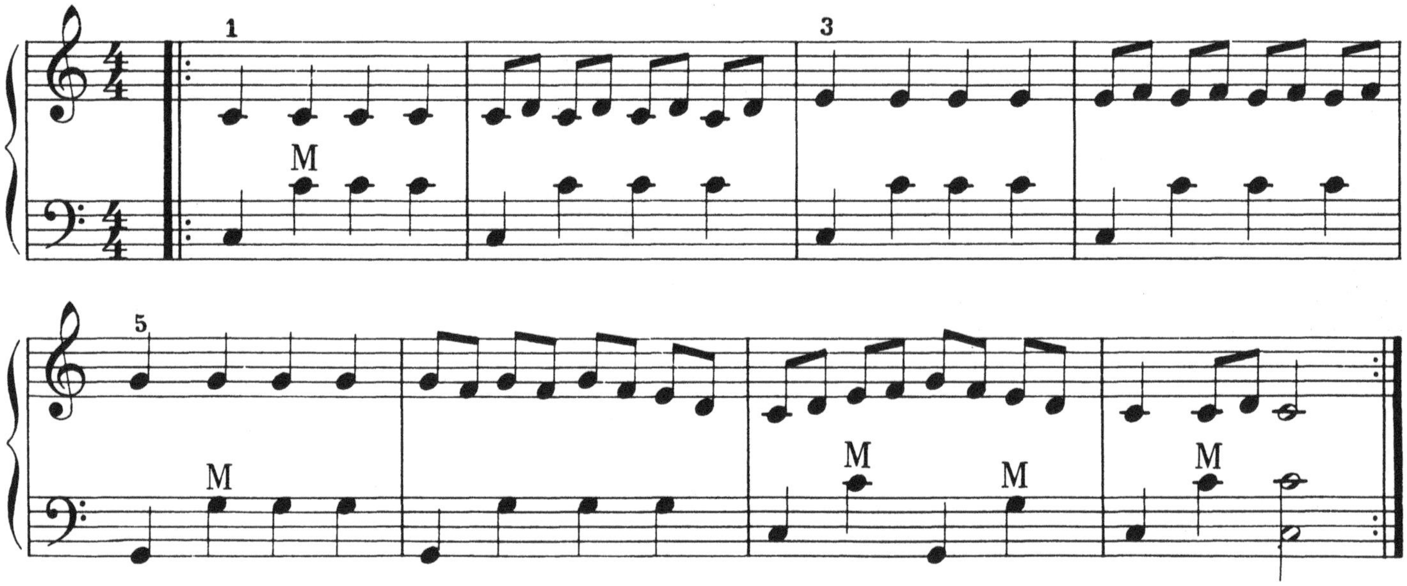

IMPORTANT! After you master the above exercise, practice it with ALTERNATING BASSES.

SPEED DRILL NO. 2

GOLDEN SLIPPERS

J. A. BLAND

Moderately fast

mf
CLAR.
BAND.
f Oh, them gold-en slip-pers! Oh, them gold-en slip-pers! Gold-en slippers I'm
gon-na wear, be-cause they look so neat.
Oh, them gold-en slippers! Oh, them
gold-en slippers! Gold-en slippers I'm gon-na wear to walk the gold-en street.

THE MAJOR SCALE

A major scale is a series of EIGHT notes in ALPHABETICAL ORDER. You have already played the C MAJOR SCALE:

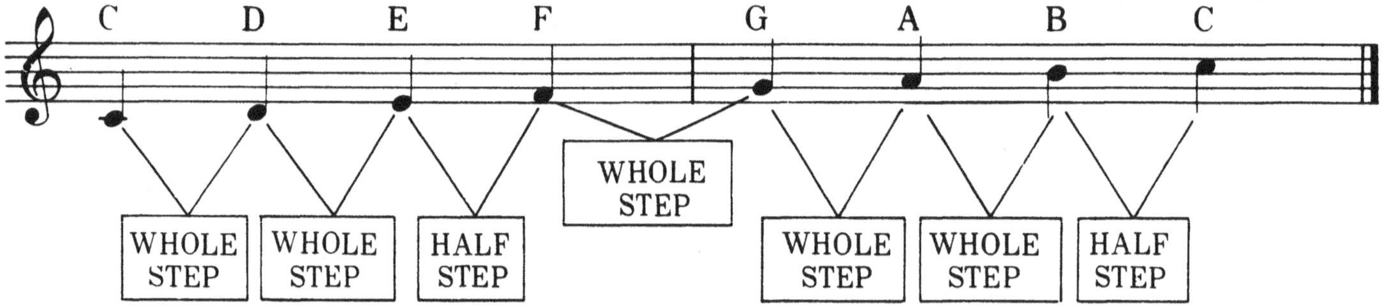

Notice that the scale above can be divided into two parts, each having the same pattern: WHOLE STEP – WHOLE STEP – HALF STEP. We call these parts TETRACHORDS.

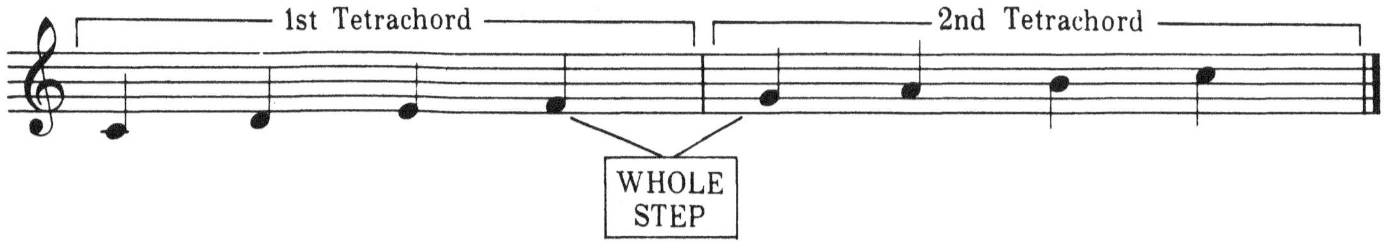

The two tetrachords are separated by a WHOLE STEP.

A MAJOR SCALE may be built starting on ANY NOTE, black or white. Using the TETRACHORD pattern, write a MAJOR SCALE, starting on G:

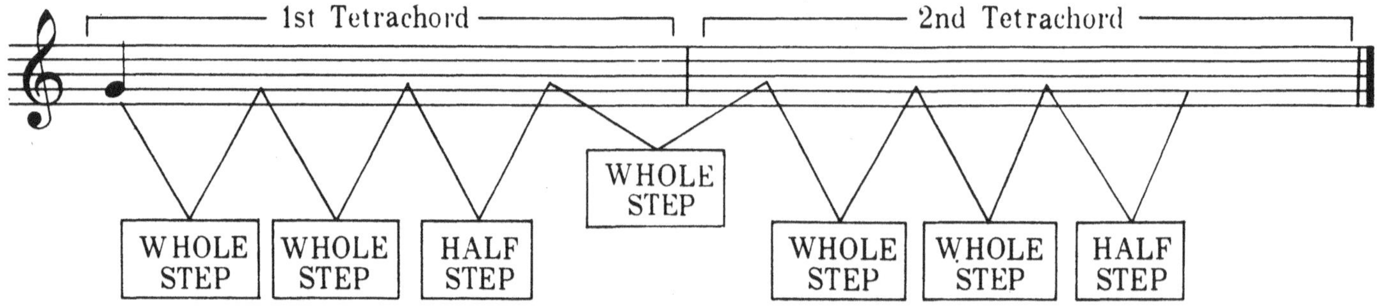

Write a MAJOR SCALE, starting on F:

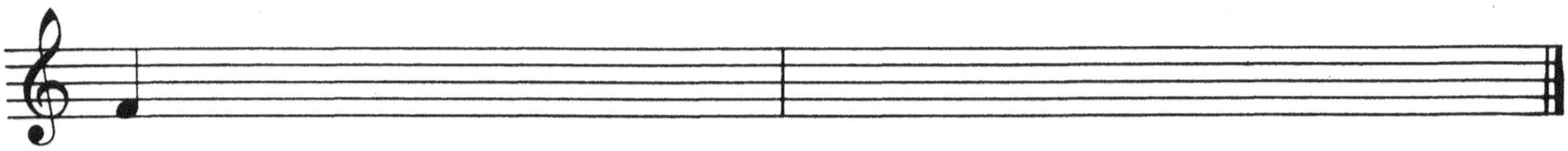

CHECK: Are the notes in alphabetical order?

KEY SIGNATURES

The KEY of C MAJOR:

A piece based on the C MAJOR SCALE is in the KEY OF C MAJOR. Since there are no sharps or flats in the C scale, any sharps or flats occuring in a piece in the KEY OF C MAJOR are called ACCIDENTALS.

The KEY of G MAJOR:

A piece based on the G MAJOR SCALE is in the KEY OF G MAJOR. Since F is sharp in the G scale, every F will be sharp in the key of G major. Instead of making all the F's sharp in the piece, the sharp is indicated at the beginning, in the KEY SIGNATURE. Sharps or flats shown in the KEY SIGNATURE are effective throughout the piece.

The KEY of F MAJOR:

A piece based on the F MAJOR SCALE is in the KEY OF F MAJOR. The key signature is ONE FLAT (Bb).

If sharps, flats, or naturals not shown in the key signature occur in the piece, they are called ACCIDENTALS
ACCIDENTALS are effective only for the measures in which they appear.

The three scales shown above should be practiced every day. Students who do this should have little difficulty playing selections written in C MAJOR, G MAJOR, and F MAJOR.

Key of F MAJOR
Key Signature
ONE FLAT (B♭).
Play all "B's"
Flat, throughout.

CHIAPANECAS

MEXICAN HAND-CLAPPING SONG

TRADITIONAL

Brightly

1. (1st time only)
NATURAL
2. (2nd time only)

INTRODUCING DOTTED QUARTER NOTES

A DOT increases the length of a note ONE-HALF!

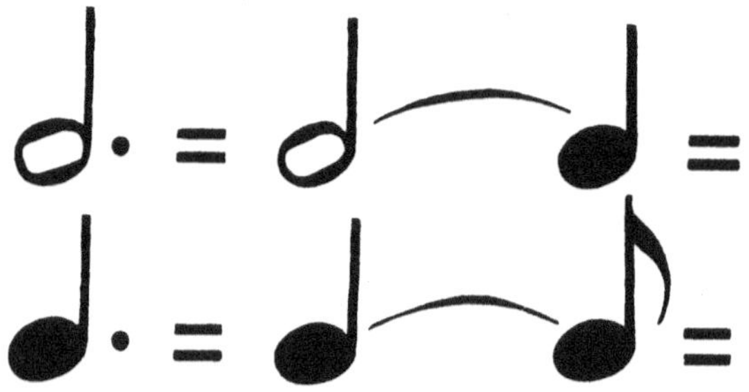

3 COUNTS

1½ COUNTS

PREPARATORY DRILL:

The only difference in the following three measures and those directly above them is the way they are written. They should sound the SAME.

COUNTRY GARDENS

Key of C MAJOR
Key signature
No SHARPS, No FLATS

ENGLISH FOLK DANCE

Moderately fast

* *f* - *p* = Forte the first time, piano the second time.

INTRODUCING MINOR CHORDS

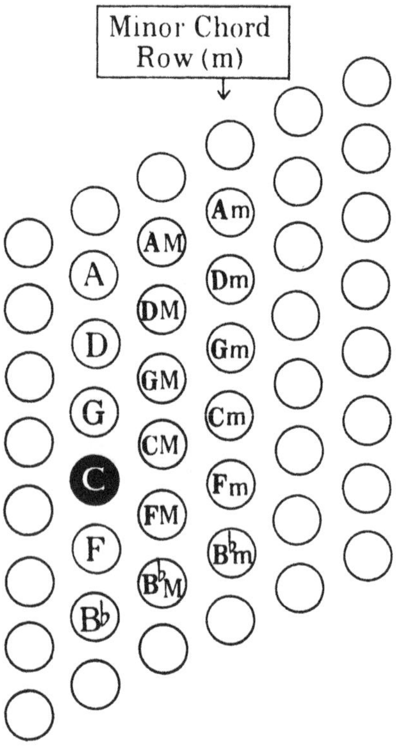

The row of buttons just after the major chord row is called the MINOR CHORD ROW.

MINOR CHORDS are indicated by a small "m" over the note.

MINKA

Moderately Slow

TRADITIONAL

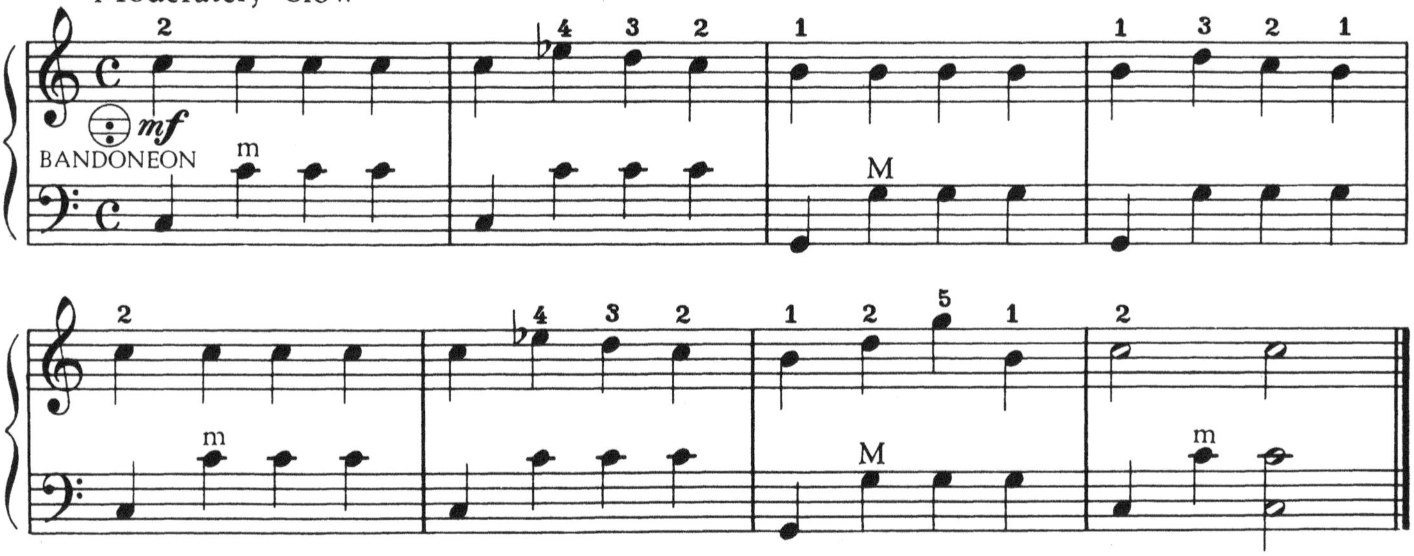

ALTERNATING BASSES WITH MINOR CHORDS

THE MERRY WIDOW

WALTZ

Key of F MAJOR
Key signature
ONE FLAT (B♭)

FRANZ LEHAR

Slow Waltz time

Gliss: Abbreviation for the word "GLISSANDO", which means "SLIDING." Using the nail of the third finger, slide over all of the white keys between the two notes indicated.

SPEED DRILL NO. 3

INTRODUCING SEVENTH CHORDS

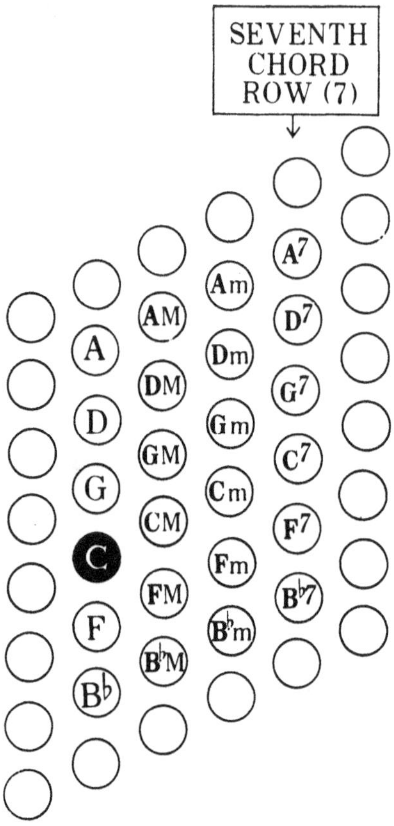

The row of buttons just after the minor chord row is called the SEVENTH CHORD ROW. SEVENTH CHORDS are indicated by the figure "7" over the note.

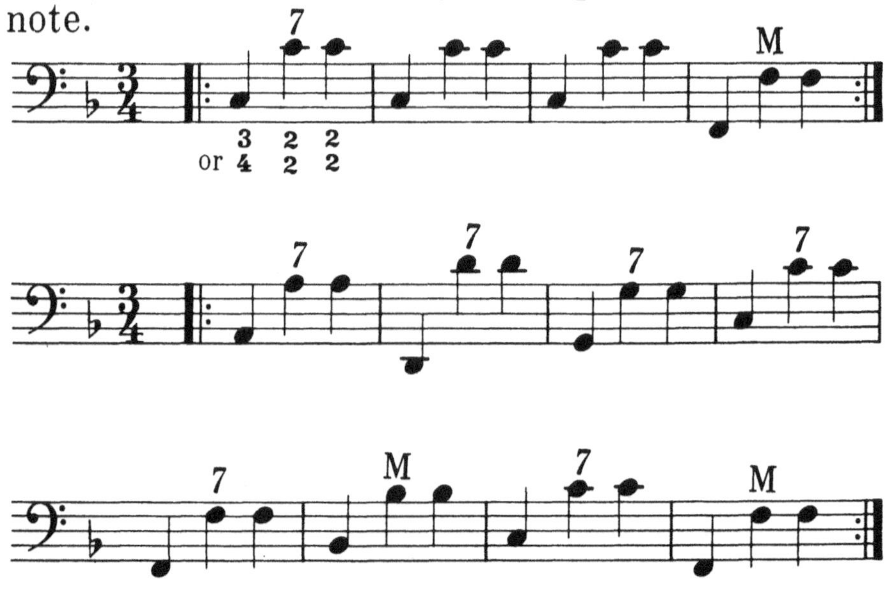

Fill in:

Key of ________
Key Signature ________

LA DONNA E MOBILE

Moderately fast

G. VERDI

COUNTY FAIR

(VARSOUVIANA)

Key of Key Signature

Moderately fast

FOLK DANCE

f
mf
f

ARABIAN ENCHANTMENT

(SCHEHERAZADE)

Key of __________
Key signature:
____

Moderately slow

RIMSKY-KORSAKOFF

⌒ HOLD SIGN (Fermata): This sign indicates that the time value of the note is lengthened (approximately twice its usual value).

INTRODUCING A, B, and C ABOVE THE STAFF

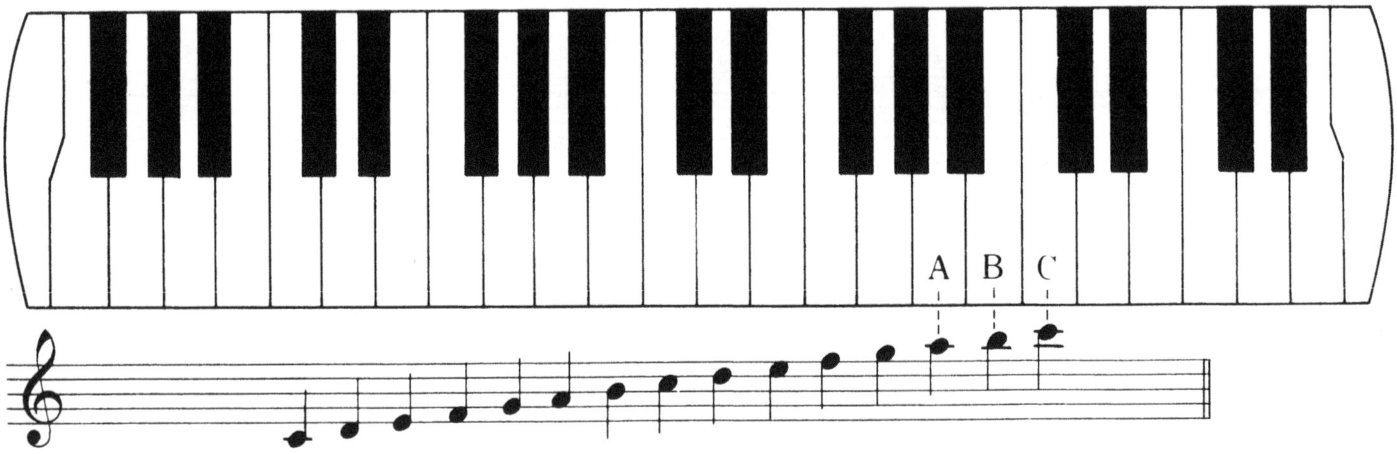

To write notes above and below the staff, we use short ADDED LINES, called LEGER LINES.

The Two Octave C Scale:
This scale should be practiced DAILY.

SPEED DRILL NO. 4

Key of ________
Key Signature:
____

ARKANSAS TRAVELER

SQUARE DANCE

DANUBE WAVES

S. IVANOVICI

To next strain
2.
3.
gliss.
8va
ritard.
Fine
D. C. al Fine

MATCHING TEST

( ) Hold Sign (Fermata)	1. >
( ) Tied Notes	2. ♭
( ) Slurred Notes	3. *f*
( ) Repeat Signs	4. ♩.
( ) Accent Mark	5. Ritard
( ) Quarter Rest	6. Common Time
( ) Whole Rest	7. Glissando
( ) Half Rest	8. 
( ) Same as 4/4 Time	9. ♯
( ) Key Signature of G Major	10. Whole Step - Whole Step - Half Step
( ) Key Signature of F Major	11. 
( ) Raises a note 1/2 Step	12. 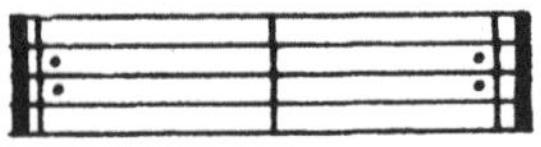
( ) Lowers a note 1/2 Step	13. 8va
( ) Cancels a Sharp or Flat	14. 𝄽
( ) Loud	15. One Sharp (F#)
( ) Soft	16. 𝄐
( ) Pattern of a tetrachord	17. 𝄒
( ) Crescendo (Gradually Louder)	18. ♫ ♪
( ) Decrescendo (Gradually Softer)	19. 
( ) Gradually Slower	20. 𝄼
( ) Sliding	21. One Flat (B♭)
( ) Shift markings	22. ♮
( ) Eighth Notes	23. 𝄓
( ) Gets one and one-half Counts	24. *p*
( ) Play one Octave Higher Than Written	25. 𝄻

GRADE____________________. (Score 4 Points for each correct answer. Passing Grade is 80.)